INDIANA PACERS
ALL-TIME GREATS

BY STEPH GIEDD

Copyright © 2024 by Press Room Editions. All rights reserved. No part of this book may be used or reproduced in any manner whatsoever, including internet usage, without written permission from the copyright owner, except in the case of brief quotations embodied in critical articles and reviews.

Book design by Jake Slavik
Cover design by Jake Slavik

Photographs ©: Darron Cummings/AP Images, cover (top), 1 (top); Tom Strattman/AP Images, cover (bottom), 1 (bottom), 14; AP Images, 4, 6; Elise Amendola/AP Images, 8; Kathy Willens/AP Images, 10; Peter Morgan/AP Images, 13; Kirby Lee/AP Images, 16; Alex Brandon/AP Images, 19, 20

Press Box Books, an imprint of Press Room Editions.

ISBN
978-1-63494-662-9 (library bound)
978-1-63494-686-5 (paperback)
978-1-63494-733-6 (epub)
978-1-63494-710-7 (hosted ebook)

Library of Congress Control Number: 2022919259

Distributed by North Star Editions, Inc.
2297 Waters Drive
Mendota Heights, MN 55120
www.northstareditions.com

Printed in the United States of America
Mankato, MN
082023

ABOUT THE AUTHOR

Steph Giedd is a former high school English teacher turned sports editor. Originally from southern Iowa, Steph now lives in Minneapolis with her husband, daughter, and pets.

TABLE OF CONTENTS

CHAPTER 1
ON PACE TO BE GREAT 4

CHAPTER 2
REGGIE MILLER TIME 10

CHAPTER 3
KEEPING THE PACE 16

TIMELINE 22
TEAM FACTS 23
MORE INFORMATION 23
GLOSSARY 24
INDEX 24

LEWIS
14

CHAPTER 1
ON PACE TO BE GREAT

The Indiana Pacers played their first season in 1967–68. But it wasn't in the NBA. Their first nine seasons were in the American Basketball Association (ABA).

One of the first great Pacers was point guard **Freddie Lewis**. He was a clutch player. Lewis often played better in the playoffs than in the regular season. **Roger Brown** provided scoring. The 6'5" small forward averaged 18.0 points per game in eight seasons in Indiana. His quickness made him tough for opponents to guard.

DANIELS
34

Mel Daniels racked up many awards during his time with the Pacers. "Big Mel" was a six-time All-Star. And he was the ABA Most Valuable Player (MVP) twice. Daniels grabbed 16.0 rebounds per game in his six seasons with the Pacers. More importantly, he combined with Lewis and Brown to win three ABA championships.

Adding more great rebounding for the Pacers was 6'8" forward **George McGinnis**. McGinnis could also score in bunches. He averaged 29.8 points per game in 1974–75. That was the most in the ABA.

STAT SPOTLIGHT

REBOUNDS PER GAME IN A SEASON
PACERS TEAM RECORD
Mel Daniels: 18.0 (1970–71)

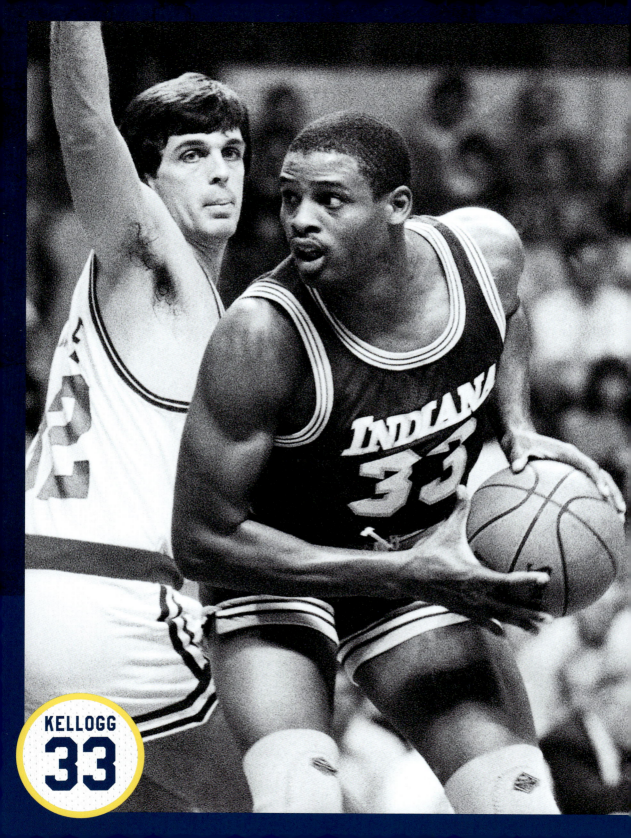

The Pacers joined the NBA for the 1976–77 season. Swingman **Billy Knight** was an All-Star right away. He averaged more than 18 points per game in eight seasons as a Pacer. And he made more than 50 percent of his shots, too. Power forward **Clark Kellogg** had an immediate impact in 1982–83. Kellogg averaged a double-double and was named to the All-Rookie Team. He was one of the best Pacers in the 1980s. But the team was about to add a future NBA superstar.

ABA LEGEND
Hall of Fame coach Bobby "Slick" Leonard led the Pacers to five ABA Finals. He came out with three championships in 1970, 1972, and 1973. Leonard also led the team to an ABA-record 69 playoff wins. After retirement, he became a popular broadcaster for the team.

CHAPTER 2
REGGIE MILLER TIME

The Pacers struggled to have success in the NBA. That started to change when they drafted **Reggie Miller** in 1987. The shooting guard spent his entire 18-year career in Indiana. Miller was a lethal three-point shooter. He made 2,560 in his career. That was the most in NBA history when he retired. In 2000, Miller's scoring led the Pacers to their first NBA Finals.

STAT SPOTLIGHT

CAREER POINTS
PACERS TEAM RECORD

Reggie Miller: 25,279

Miller was also known for his trash talk. So was forward **Chuck Person**. He annoyed his opponents by insulting them. And he backed it up with his skill. "The Rifleman" won the Rookie of the Year in 1986–87. Forward **Detlef Schrempf** was traded to the Pacers in 1989. He provided scoring off the bench for Indiana. That earned him the Sixth Man of the Year Award twice. The award is given to the best player off the bench each season.

QUICK TURNAROUND

Miller's signature moment came in a 1995 playoff game in New York against the Knicks. The Pacers were losing Game 1 by six points with 18.7 seconds left. Miller then scored eight points in less than nine seconds of game time. The Pacers won the game by two. They went on to win the series in seven games.

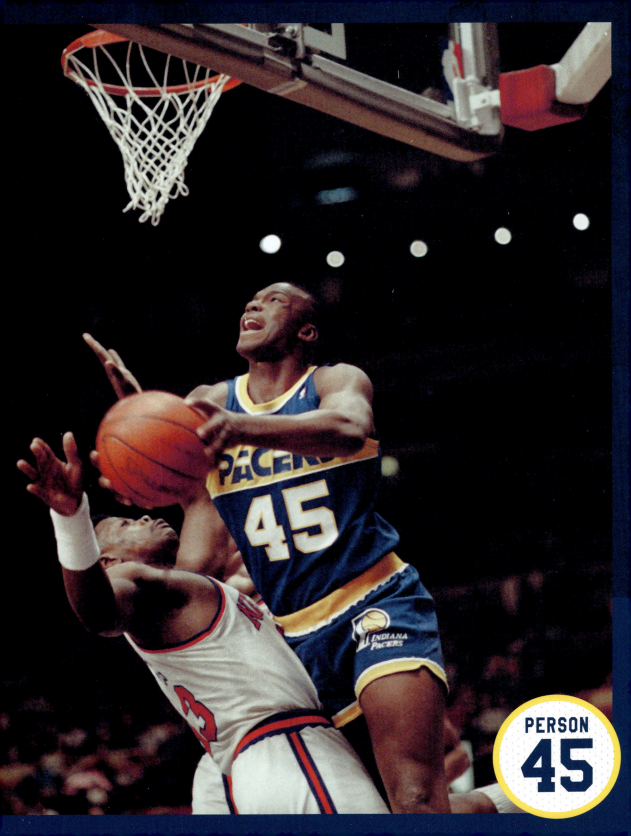

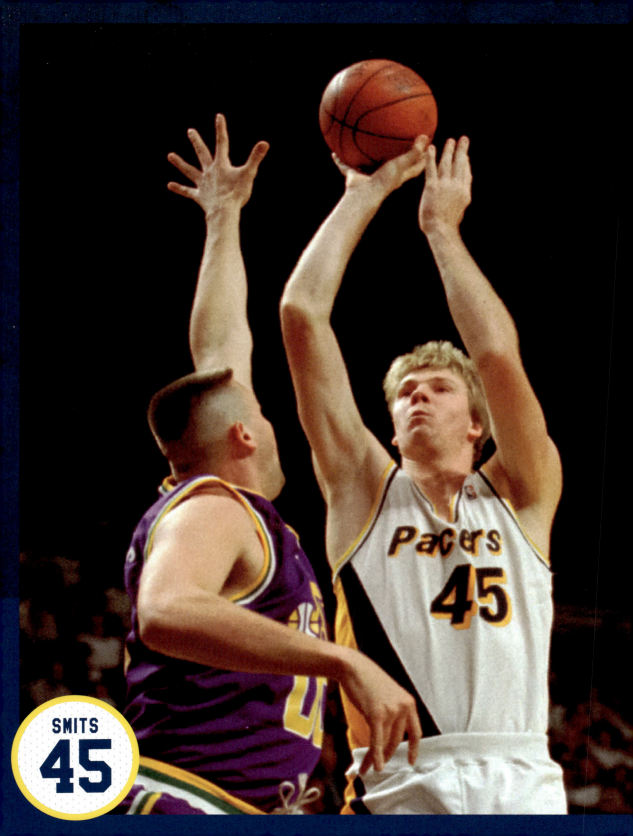

Like Miller, center **Rik Smits** played his whole career for the Pacers. "The Dunking Dutchman" stood 7'4". Despite the nickname, he was best known for his hook shot. Few defenders were tall enough to block his attempts. Smits's biggest shot came in the 1995 Eastern Conference Finals against the Orlando Magic. He hit a buzzer-beater to win Game 4 and tie the series 2–2.

The Pacers didn't need **Dale Davis** to score. The 6'11" big man hustled all the time. And he outworked a lot of players. He often guarded the opposing team's best scorer. That helped the Pacers consistently make the playoffs in the 1990s.

CHAPTER 3
KEEPING THE PACE

The Pacers still had Reggie Miller in the early 2000s. But they needed a new star. They found one when they traded for big man **Jermaine O'Neal** in 2000. O'Neal helped the Pacers make the playoffs in six of his eight seasons with the team. He also made the All-Star team six straight years during that stretch.

Small forward **Ron Artest** joined the Pacers a year after O'Neal. Artest was a physical defender. That earned him the Defensive Player of the Year Award in 2003–04.

Artest was traded in 2006. After that, the Pacers missed the playoffs for four seasons in a row. That changed when small forward **Paul George** joined the team. George was known for his defense when he first entered the league in 2010–11. Then he developed into an elite scorer. George led the Pacers to the conference finals in 2013 and 2014.

The Pacers traded George before the 2017–18 season. They got shooting guard **Victor Oladipo** in return. The former Indiana University star looked right

LARRY LEGEND

Larry Bird was a Hall of Fame player for the Boston Celtics. But he grew up in Indiana. He joined the Pacers as the head coach in 1997. "Larry Legend" retired from coaching after the 2000 NBA Finals run. Bird then came back in 2003 to work in Indiana's front office. He held a role with the team until he stepped down in 2022.

at home with the Pacers. His 2.4 steals per game led the league in 2017–18. And he was an All-Star his first two seasons with the team. The Pacers made the playoffs all three full seasons Oladipo was there.

Center **Myles Turner** was a big reason why, too. Turner made it hard for opposing teams to score in the paint. He led the league in blocks per game in two different seasons. Turner and a young core are giving Pacers fans hope for the future.

STAT SPOTLIGHT

BLOCKS PER GAME IN A SEASON
PACERS TEAM RECORD
Myles Turner: 3.4 (2020-21)

TIMELINE

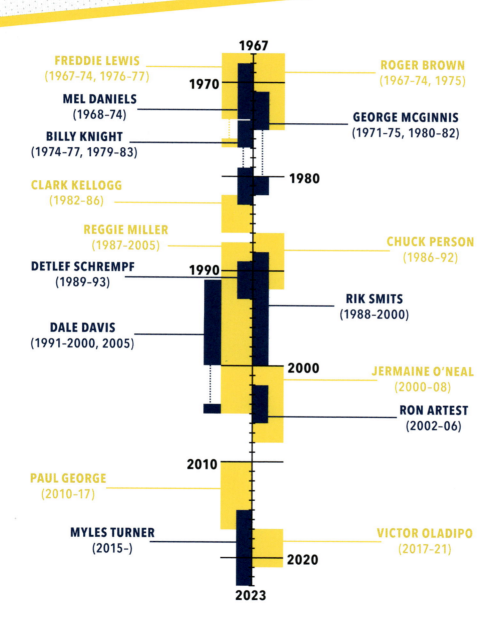

TEAM FACTS

INDIANA PACERS

First season: 1967-68

NBA championships: 0*

Key coaches:

Larry Bird (1997-98 to 1999-2000)
147-67, 32-20 playoffs

Bobby "Slick" Leonard (1968-69 to 1979-80)
387-270, 69-47 playoffs

Frank Vogel (2011 to 2015-16)
250-181, 31-30 playoffs

MORE INFORMATION

To learn more about the Indiana Pacers, go to **pressboxbooks.com/AllAccess**.

These links are routinely monitored and updated to provide the most current information available.

*Through 2021-22 season

GLOSSARY

clutch
Successful late in games or in pressure-filled situations.

conference
A smaller group of teams that make up part of a sports league.

double-double
When a player reaches 10 or more of two different statistics in a game.

draft
To select in an event that allows teams to choose new players coming into the league.

elite
The best of the best.

front office
The team's management.

hook shot
A one-handed shot in which a player extends one arm out to the side and over their head toward the basket.

lethal
Deadly.

paint
Another term for the lane, the area between the basket and the free throw line.

rookie
A first-year player.

INDEX

Artest, Ron, 17–18

Bird, Larry, 18
Brown, Roger, 5, 7

Daniels, Mel, 7
Davis, Dale, 15

George, Paul, 18

Kellogg, Clark, 9
Knight, Billy, 9

Leonard, Bobby "Slick," 9
Lewis, Freddie, 5, 7

McGinnis, George, 7
Miller, Reggie, 11–12, 15, 17

Oladipo, Victor, 18, 21
O'Neal, Jermaine, 17

Person, Chuck, 12

Schrempf, Detlef, 12
Smits, Rik, 15

Turner, Myles, 21

24